SUZANNE STABILE

THE
PATH
BETWEEN
US

JOURNAL

An imprint of InterVarsity Press
Downers Grove, Illinois

InterVarsity Press
P.O. Box 1400, Downers Grove, IL 60515-1426
ivpress.com
email@ivpress.com

InterVarsity Press® is the book-publishing division of InterVarsity Christian Fellowship/USA®, a movement of students and faculty active on campus at hundreds of universities, colleges, and schools of nursing in the United States of America, and a member movement of the International Fellowship of Evangelical Students. For information about local and regional activities, visit intervarsity.org.

Cover design and image composite: David Fassett
Interior design: Daniel van Loon
Images: Wavy line background: ©Kalisson/iStock/Getty Images
     People walking: ©Ricardo Dias/EyeEm/Getty Images

ISBN 978-0-8308-4681-8 (print)

Printed in the United States of America ∞

InterVarsity Press is committed to ecological stewardship and to the conservation of natural resources in all our operations. This book was printed using sustainably sourced paper.

Library of Congress Cataloging-in-Publication Data
A catalog record for this book is available from the Library of Congress.

P	21	20	19	18	17	16	15	14	13	12	11	10	9	8	7	6	5	4	3	2	1
Y	37	36	35	34	33	32	31	30	29	28	27	26	25	24	23	22	21	20			

> You can't change how you see. You can only change *what you do* with how you see.

All relationships—
those that truly
matter and even
those that don't—
require translation.
And if our interest
in relational growth
and transformation
is sincere, then
the Enneagram is
one of the most
helpful translation
tools available.

In my experience there are two things we have in common: we all want to belong, and we all want our lives to have meaning.

Looking through
the lens of the
Enneagram makes
it possible to better
understand ourselves
and others, increase
our acceptance
and compassion,
and navigate the
paths between us.

It's important to remember that the Enneagram is not a static system: we are all moving from healthy, through average, to unhealthy, and back again. In my experience, most of us spend our time somewhere in the high-average range.

The Enneagram teaches you who you are not. Your personality is actually covering who you are, but you can't make it through at least the first half of life without it.

Please don't use your Enneagram number as an excuse for your behavior.

Don't use what you've learned about the other numbers to make fun of, criticize, stereotype, or in any way disrespect them. It would be great if you would spend your energy observing and working on yourself as opposed to observing and working on others.

When we are able to
see ourselves as we
are, and as we can be,
it is a beautiful thing.

The Enneagram
teaches us that
the nine ways we
deal with crisis
are both habitual
and predictable.

Discernment is usually more reliable when we give consideration to the entirety of our relationships. It's damaging, regardless of Enneagram number, when we get lost in the highs and lows.

As we gain an appreciation for the gifts each of us bring to the table, along with the limitations and problems that are associated with each of the nine numbers, we are capable of offering ourselves, and the world, far more compassion.

The Enneagram is always helpful. If there is something not helpful regarding the number you go to in stress, or another move on the Enneagram, then you're misunderstanding the system.

While it's never wise to guess at or assign Enneagram numbers to other people, we can honor the differences between us and the people we love by learning about the other eight Enneagram numbers.

Our tendency is to believe we can do anything if we work hard enough, but that isn't true when talking about personality. Willpower is a myth that is fueled by emotion, and it will not serve you well in dealing with your Enneagram number.

Motivation is at the heart of the Enneagram. In fact, the key to understanding all Enneagram wisdom is to remember that a person's Enneagram number is determined by his or her motivation and not by behavior.

When we move too fast, when we don't think, and when we fail to consider feelings—ours and others'— we make decisions based on the things that motivate us in our personality.

Our fears, whether we are aware of them or not, can have a significant impact on how we relate to others.

We want to belong in a group or to another person, and we want to believe that our presence has some kind of value. But it's a struggle when we have to manage our anxiety about not being enough.

Healthy relationships
depend on our
understanding
that there are nine
ways of seeing the
world, nine ways
of processing what
we see, and nine
ways of deciding
how to proceed.

Every number
struggles with
something and
experiences
significant pain—
they just struggle
with different
things. As we grow
in awareness, our
compassion and
empathy increase,
and we're able to
extend more grace
to one another.

You can't build community if every person's thinking has to be the same.

Habits are hard to change—and personality is formed around habitual, predictable, mechanical responses to life. To change all of it requires a great deal of awareness and personal work.

Your Enneagram number is well-honed by the time you are five, so be patient with yourself in trying to allow parts of it to fall away.

We cannot do soul work with dualistic thinking. When we ask questions of mentors, spiritual directors, and advisors, generally what we're asking for is support for the answers that we already have. If we aren't open to new answers, we grow our personalities, not our souls.

One of the reasons it's so important to me that people learn the Enneagram is that this wisdom helps us to choose a reaction. And when we don't know the Enneagram, reactions often choose us.

You have no right
to expect people
to treat you a
certain way if you
haven't requested it.

Personality is not a lie. It's what is required of us as children to make it in the world. And it's a good thing—until it isn't.

I think every number reflects healthy spirituality in some way. And I believe people who are healthy can teach us that there is something transcendent even in the most boring moments.

When aggressive numbers don't respect authority, they become the authority. That's problematic because it's often not their place.

Lots of relationship
struggles happen
because we don't
have enough
respect for context.
People are easy
to see—they're
in the forefront.
Context is difficult
to see because
it's the backdrop.
Relationships are
usually damaged
when we ignore
context.

It's very easy to recognize other people's weaknesses based on your own strengths. But it can be very difficult to realize your own weaknesses through the same lens.

We need to learn to avoid assigning hurt in a relationship to an Enneagram number. It's best to assign hurt to a person, and work with that in the relationship. With every Enneagram number, this offers a more respectful approach to relationships.

The only thing that's dangerous about the Enneagram is that we take it to be more than it is. It's just one spiritual wisdom tool, and it's better when considered alongside other traditional spiritual practices.

The Enneagram is not reductive. In fact, it is quite expansive when properly understood and applied.

You can't change what you can't name. The Enneagram helps you name the behavior that doesn't serve you well. It's always good to try to be honest with yourself, but it's never easy.

The Enneagram doesn't put you in a box. It shows you the box you're already in.

If you are working
with the Enneagram
in a healthy way—
and for the right
reasons—then you
will learn to allow
personality to
fall away, making
room for more of
your true self.

Never tell anyone what their Enneagram number is. First, because you don't know. And second, because you rob them of the journey.

The Enneagram shows you where your weaknesses are *and* how to fix them—at exactly the same time.

ALSO AVAILABLE

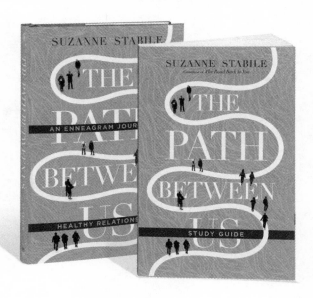

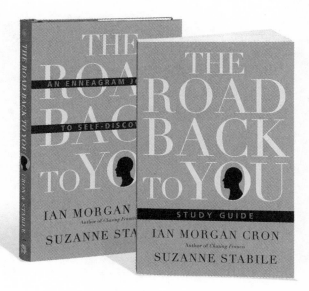